D0934213

NEW WORLD ARCHITECTURE

NEW WORLD ARCHITECTURE

Poems by Matthew Graham

Published by The Galileo Press   Baltimore   1985

Grateful acknowledgement is made to the editors of the publications in which the following poems first appeared:

The Antioch Review: "To a Friend Killed in the Fighting, Dominican Republic, 1965"
On Turtle's Back: A Bio-Geographic Anthology of New York State Poets: "Christmas, Tonjes Farm: Callicoon, New York"
Dancy: "King Fish," "Working the River"
Kansas Quarterly: "Matthew Brady Speaks of Whitman"
The Missouri Review: "Union Town"
Nit and Wit: "My Father," "Factory"
Open Places: "The American Falls," "Kitchen," "At the Wayne County Fair"
Pavement: "Moving November"
Poet and Critic: "Translation"
The Pushcart Prize VII: "Translation"
The Reaper: "Helicopters," "Hank Williams Still Life"
Tendril: "An Afternoon in Florida"

"Working the River," "California," "Helicopters," "At the Bridge of the Prairie Du Chien," and "At the Wayne County Fair" first appeared in a limited-edition chapbook, *Hanging on the Sunburned Arm of Some Homeboy,* Domino Impressions (Iowa City, Iowa), 1982.

Cover photo by John P. Wendell, Jr.
Cover art: "Barn Raising on the Rainy River," c. 1895, Photographer unknown
Cover design by Jack Stephens

ISBN 0-913123-07-2 (cloth)
ISBN 0-913123-05-6 (paperback)

Library of Congress Catalog Card Number 84-81137

First Edition

Published by The Galileo Press, 15201 Wheeler Lane, Sparks, Maryland 21152

For Fred Madeo,
For Leslie Adrienne Miller

Contents

One was brought to a peculiar consciousness of
what it meant to be at home in America . . .
                                    – Edmund Wilson
                                    Memoirs of Hecate County

PART ONE

To A Friend Killed in the Fighting: Dominican Republic, 1965

Imagine this: We are spaced beside the road
Like the five spikes of the red morning star
That I can just see now in the east.
Or we are the thin cracks in the bottom
Of the blue porcelain cup my grandmother used
To make me herb tea when I was sick, as a child.

I am sick now without you. This road
Is the same road where years ago you herded
Your father's useless cows. At dawn we expect
An American convoy; and although I do not like
The word ambush, it is the only one left
In my vocabulary. I imagine how much

They will be surprised. Remember we once
Joked, that when we die we will go to America.
Well now I think we only return here,
Back to this island floating like smoke on the sea,
This warm wreckage, these repeating movements where
The night is too long without you. It is your breath

On my cheek, your touch, the dusty roadside
Flowers I wanted to cover you with
Only there was not time. Two nights ago
I snuck into town to see that woman.
My friend, I am sorry but she loved
Too many men, she tried too hard to

Come between us; and when she called me by your name
In the night, I should have broken her neck like a bird's.
The black night is so long it could be the wind.
The others are stationed around me and we
Communicate in whistles. Tell me, my friend,
What you feel now. Whistle a soft song

3

So I can forget the hour. Hold me once
More in this world that has been measured
In calibers, that is quartered by crosshairs
And defined by what enters them,
Once more before I step onto the road,
In sunlight, your stolen automatic rifle

In my hands.

Christmas, Tonjes Farm: Callicoon, New York
(for Jordan Smith)

Pastoral Americana. This is calendar country
Rerouted through gullies of washed-out earth
That first snow has covered.
I watch from the barnyard as the sweep of hills
And parts of the house turn a dead red.
The sun moves down a cold road leaving
Nothing but a hum in the power lines
And the smell of ham in the blue wood smoke.
This is the lip-splitting cold of closed creameries
And long whistles. It turns the blood inward,
Washing over dry weeds and keeping in mind
These hard-worked hills, as if this murmur
Of the end of the year was meant
To move the stalled skulls of cows,
And lie in the roots of uncut corn.
I let it settle like ice in the lake.
It takes time to remember the taste
Of bruised light trapped here in winter.
Yet when the owl my friend keeps in the barn
Screeches for something else, it all comes home
Like the snap of bone deep in the woods
Where shadows cross and double cross.

Moving November

I first learned to drive on a tractor, when I was ten,
An old Allis-Chalmers that belonged to my grandfather.
The clutch was so strong that my leg shook

Each time I tried to hold it down. The gears jammed
And the engine sputtered oil in the cold upstate
New York drizzle at the end of corn cutting season.

But I learned to drive and it left me
With admiration for all things that move. The trucks
On the interstate, the grind of the seasons,

The vast drag of this midwestern sky that I passed under
Three years ago, hitchhiking toward Colorado
And a possible job. This midwest.

Back here, broke and stuck, I begin to feel a panic
Build up like the mumble of vowels in my throat
When I pronounce the name of this state.

Yesterday, as we walked across a corn-stubbled field,
I remembered the fields of my grandfather
And all those long dusty cuts

Of November; a friend who hung himself
In a shed, men gathered before dawn
To drag the lake, and the last scream

Of geese along the swamp.
As we walked toward a collapsing barn collecting
The last light you held me and asked

What I was thinking. I should have said
That your blond hair is the color of these fields
In summer. That your eyes hold the confines of both

The edges of the sky and the dark parts of the building
We are about to enter. That I could teach you
To drive even though a woman can make a sound

That can stop a tractor four acres away.
All I could say was I'll follow you
Inside. Winter is coming and I'm already moving.

The American Falls

I hold my grandmother's paperweight
And feel in it the cold
Of this new winter. Lying below the surface
Of the heavy convex glass,
Is a sepia photograph of Niagara Falls –
Distorted, billowed,
And in certain light
Pouring out over my hand.
The mist in the distance
Rises on the rim of another country,
And I wonder which spring train ride
From Rochester to the Falls
Sixty some years ago,
Was the reason for this memento.

One winter I hitchhiked on I-90
Across the Niagara Frontier
To be able to sit with a shy girl
In a bar off Rainbow Boulevard
And watch the colored lights
Play on the spray of the American Falls.
The profile of the cliffs
Was changing then,
Falling in the night, and the spray
Froze on the dull bar windows,
On windshields and eyelashes.
Later, I stood for a whole afternoon
At the East Rochester toll with my hand raised,
While a solid stream of cars
Inched past me from the city
Of my grandmother's birth,
Through the snow with their headlights on.

I've often looked for two figures
By the railing at the top
Of the falls inside the paperweight

That might be my grandmother and a young man
I once saw in her photo album.
The picture was taken on the edge
Of the Cave of the Winds wooden walkway,
My grandmother's dark hair is down
And blown back away from the white stem
Of her neck. She is laughing
Above the roar of the water,
And her companion's face is shadowed
By the brim of his straw boater.
Beneath the picture she had written
In a script that concealed
Her hard Canadian vowels,
"April 1917 – Smile, and the whole world . . ."

I always wanted to believe
That the smile would justify
The young man's tightrope walking
Or barrel riding over the American Falls
In the name of love or pride
Or other adventures that the whole world then,
In its brown and white simplicity,
Would applaud.
In truth that smile brought her
The weight of Niagara,
A constant falling boundary,
An insistence to pass on,
To hold down the lists
And the recipes, the bills,
The letters he would never write.

In The Promised Land

Spring stuns my part of town
Like a window shade sprung open
And left flapping in an unfurnished sublet.
Clotheslines and jonquils appear in the short yards
Of warm air between the duplexes, and from speakers
Propped in a window a woman laments
A man who won't stop being a muchacho.
All kinds of trash blossoms
In the mud of my yard,
Including my neighbor's ass end, protruding
From the open hood of his Olds 88.
I smell the air through the screen and think of the wind
In the mountain fields of my home.
Each spring before plowing
I worked rocks from the mire of those fields
And piled them in random monuments to the wind
That whittled everything back
To raw essentials.
When I was a kid I had ambition.
At sixteen I bought a used Ford Falcon
And drove out from all that,
But spring comes back with its whole subdivision
Of promise, and I wonder how other men
Wade through their lives
Along the frontiers of their patios,
Here in Poco Paraiso.
How far the sons have come
From their fathers' farms.

My Father

I think my father wears his brother's death
Like the upstate winters that are finally getting to him.
His brother disappeared in a thunderclap
Over France and saved my father
From the war. Who was he to forgive –
His own father who hammered at them both
From milking time to milking time until someone
Had to break?
I can only think my father may still walk in shadows
Larger than his own cast roughly
Over thirty-seven years he never asked for.
When he was young he once helped to build
A great dam until the night four men
Dropped eighty feet and my father walked away.
He calls me lucky.
He calls me nigger rich
And complains he can't find a good 25 dollar car anymore.
He could have hitchhiked anywhere.
He could have smiled up a fortune with the smile
I've seen in a picture he has
Taken near the end of the war
In a Times Square bar, on a Saturday.
My father and two friends, all in uniform,
Raise their glasses in a gesture of arrogant
Indifference, so popular then.
I've looked at that picture a lot.
I've tried to find something of myself
In what he was before I knew him. Something in his face
That might explain how he was able to smile
So hesitantly, so soon.
I hang around Times Square sometimes
And try to wear my restlessness like a regulation
Dress coat from the 1940's. I try to see
As he did, past the bus station
And ruined marquees, but the chances I take
Are nothing to the refuge he's built

In being the one left behind.
I don't see my father much.
He dislikes the city and doesn't visit.
I could never afford to leave.

New World Architecture

Part of the ceiling has collapsed
In the main dining room
On Ellis Island.
Bits of lathing and plaster
Mixed with horsehair
Cover the tables, the porcelain
And the tin.
On the walls are the old signs
In Russian and Yiddish.
Sunlight lies warm and dusty
By the high windows
Along the hallway of lockers
Still holding unclaimed luggage.
A slate staircase leads to the upper ruins
Where they changed the names.
Outside a white ship slides
Against the stone quay.

From here the skyline of the city
Could be a description memorized
From a letter. A language
That can't contain what it built —
The story of buildings. The towers of sky
Where no one sleeps. The boundaries of wind
As melodic as streetcars
Climbing Lower Broadway toward Canal,
The circling landaus in the shadows
Of cathedrals. A whisper of laundry, smoke,
The gold-toothed smile of the street.

The White Horse Tavern

During these bitter late afternoons it almost seems
To be snowing in here. I can feel a certain warmth
Turn everything white. The flakes drift down
From the high tin ceiling, filling glasses and covering
The sawdust tracks of patrons the way it covers
The broken streets outside. I like it in here.
The true cuts of heartwood frame beveled windows
That swing out in a slender arc of sincerity.
It is so sure of its elegance
In decline, unraveling from its past, turning
Slowly as the neighborhood turns, into long shadows,
Into the working class crowd at the bar.
The possibilities of the evening to come, the tenderness
And refusals, wash over the conversations.
Here, the dream does not need the approval of memory,
And it's at times like this I wish I could remember
Our number. I want to call and say listen, I can't
Come home right now, I'm not hungry.
It's warm in here and the glass is just beginning
To frost over. I can hear the traffic on Hudson Street
And see couples window-shopping. I recognize
The forced casualness in their just looking, and they
Remind me of when we visited an antique shop near here.
The front door clanged
And in the background a phone was ringing.
Among the collection of beginnings and ends you found
A doll whose untouched features might have been
A daughter's or your own as a child.
The black, silk, almost Oriental hair,
The porcelain face of absolute white, clouded in
Behind the hand-painted look
Of pure, unforgiving silence.
In the shop, while the stalled light dimmed
And the city pushed on outside, you held
The doll and rocked it until I took it
Away and said no, we can't
Afford this, it is nothing we can have.

14

After The War; When Coltrane Only Wanted To Play Dance Tunes
(for Larry Levis)

The sadness of afternoons was unmistakable.
There was no new way
Of seeing. The woman who left me
Could have returned at any time
Breathless, a strand of dark hair
Caught in the corner
Of her mouth. The dance hall of the Audubon
Still held

Its own particular style
Of forgiveness, as familiar
As the headlines of the old newspapers
Stuffed in the glory holes
Between the stalls of the downstairs toilet.

People kept their distance.
Couples two-stepped in tight circles
Among the pigeons and the dusk
And the dice games of the park.

The boys in the shadows
Were not praying,
But only tying their shoes,
And I moved in my own time,
And listened again for saxophones.

I'm quitting this place soon

Was still the tune
The girls mouthed to the gypsy
Cabs along the avenue.

Jazz

We ride all night west
Through the flat lands, beneath the Sohio signs
Of your home state.
You sleep in the passenger seat
Locked in a dream that does not include
The curve of the windshield
Or the broken line it pulls between us.
We are somewhere without a station
Until a riff of 40's bebop
Breaks through the static of the radio
And fills the cramped room of this car.
I think of the late show
At the West End Cafe in New York.
How the old men leaned into their horns.
How the notes sounded like money owed;
Notes that never said
All they wanted to say.

Hank Williams Still Life

(for Ben Reynolds)

We thought of our hard times
And drank to this new year of no jobs
And less money, these hard times

That demand so little, really,
Just the chance to start a new life
Somewhere. It snowed last night

And the snow looked the way I imagine music
Sounds to a southerner not acquainted with snow
In a time when the word train meant harmonica,

Guitar, goodbye. We think of car owners
And how good it would be to ride again
In the back seat with our feet up

Toward Nashville, a name that came straight
From the back of the heart, a city mentioned
With a sidelong glance of someone

Who hoped to have come a long way. You drop a record
On the stereo you inherited
From a drawn-out affair, and wake me

With a skipped drunken beat. I remember
We haven't been fair to ourselves.
Lately we've stopped rehearsing the chartbreakers.

We've stopped accepting the colored flags
At the used car lot,
The highway to the fairgrounds, and the fair itself;

The snowbound midway, the lean bandstand
Tallow-colored and quiet, as a sort of style
Suitable for the start of new lives.

After the Reception

Listen. There's a song
That repeats the same words
Until they become meaningless,
Or changed in meaning,
Like the dazed landscape where a man
Walks a great distance
Because he's out of time
Or luck. Or there's a song that starts
With the last train out
Of a bad night. The letter
You open in a cold room
That begins, *I'm sorry,*
And doesn't end though the words
Are only mouthed. Listen.
I can't lie to you. Once I knew,
After driving all night,
Half asleep at dawn,
That the gold band between the hills
And the sky was an image
Repeated from the past
Where all leaving and returning
Became the same,
That the sound of the car radio
Could be the confusion of glass
Spilled on the steps, the betrayed porches,
The bright fields of a wedding
Dress, boxed and stored.
Or that it could be relieved in the slow motion
Of one couple dancing alone
In a deserted barroom
Long after the chairs are stacked
And the music has stopped.

What The Waiter Promises

(for David Fenza)

It is just dusk.
A breeze from the sea stirs the canopy
Above the iron tables
And the empty bentwood chairs
That look like waiters
Drinking after-hours.
Music picks up and lanterns color
The promenade where couples stroll
Discussing which cafe to discover,
As if these places won't exist
Unless they call them their own.
I sigh in the shadows,
Sipping soda with bitters.
There will be ample time for them
To decide. I have their nights
Memorized. I could do this work
In my dreams.
In a few hours the faces will merge
Like running lights on the ships in the bay.
The demands and the reasons for them
Are always impossible; distant, fleeting gestures
Behind the glow of smiles.
I bow knowingly.
And admit only
What a waiter needs to admit —
Which bills to pad, which tables to save.
Who gets what with a twist,
Who remembers my eyes,
Who avoids them.

Chicago

I saw a man and he danced with his wife in Chicago
– Sammy Kahn
Chicago, Chicago
(as sung by Sinatra in the early 50's)

I have no memory of that Chicago,
But memory returns the way I imagine
That woman returned to the assured architecture
Of her husband's arms
And began again that dance
On the edge of love –
A formal occasion.
Perhaps a reception at the Drake they were both invited to
Separately, by mutual friends.
Friends who calculated the perfect steps for her to follow
Across the taffeta-crowded dance floor, under lavender
Lanterns and on
Into the well-worn light of a patient partner.
Perhaps she paused though, for a moment,
And looked back at the singer
So frail in his rented tux,
With a glance that might have said,
Had anyone seen it, . . . Really, I'm sorry.
Perhaps there were no friends.
Perhaps she never left her husband at all,
And this was just a small diversion
On the way to a reunion she planned for herself
To restore some of the razzmatazz,
To make the whole trial and error of an affair
Something more than the nervous fashion of a coming age
With its small cold wars, its anorexia.

When a woman left me to move back
I wished her the best, sincerely, and then I saw
How her things were not just hers anymore,
How her warm apartment became as public and cold
As a dance floor.
And her bed, like Chicago, was just another place
In this world I'd never been.

To The Confederate Women Of Baltimore

What is history, if not a chilled thought
        Brought suddenly alive
By the narrow misses our vision
        Allows? Always, what we
Do not at first remember returns,
        And although it is not
A day for history, I'm standing here
        On the corner of North
Charles and University Avenue
        Watching a statue swell
With the throb of rush hour traffic
        As if with defiance
Against one more minor disturbance
        In a long line of lost
Causes. I watch the statue carefully,
        Having come down this street
On purpose, going out of my way,
        And I notice that the
Two women are of different ages,
        The young soldier with them
Is in rags, and I do not move closer.
        The wind for a moment
Seems to shift the skirts, the hair, and the
        Eyes glisten for the dead,
Not with tears or with a reflection
        Of strength or forgiveness,
But with a softening, wrong and gone
        In this world, that beckons
Beyond the winter light, and makes me
        Remember some women
And think, as I turn to go in the
        Cold swirl of the city,
That maybe a smile cuts their thin lips;
        That the older woman
Standing by the smashed staff of the flag
        Stands for nothing but the

Protection of the young girl below
    In whose lap rests the head
Of the soldier, and whose mouth is drawn
    Toward his neck, taunting as
Always – my brother, my child, my son.

Translation

*Cao Giao flung open the door of
room C-2 in the Hotel Continental
where I had just arrived, and we
hugged each other excitedly, both of
us happy to be together again in
Saigon.*

                    – Tiziano Terzani
                    Giai Phong

Not exactly. With its airports and avenues, its awe of the
sleight of hand and all things misinterpreted – I hated that
city. It reflected only the image of a sleeping thief and liar,
and I feared that man because he was a journalist and remembered
everything. Outside the Hotel Continental two ARVN officers
emptied their automatics into each other's chests because they
were Catholics and afraid to commit suicide. I flung open the
door of room C-2 expecting a body or a bullet and received an
embrace. It was Sunday. April 27th, 1975, and I had come
up from the hard light of the delta into the smoke and
confusion the Americans had left because the journalist
needed a translator; he paid well, and this was not a time
to think of mistakes in judgement. The shelling stopped
two days later and on the early morning of the 30th the first
tank entered the city. It was covered in palm leaves
and red mud that turned to dust and smelled of the jungle.
Chickens in a wooden cage and bunches of water beets hung
from its sides. It swung left on Hong Tap Tu street and
stopped a girl on a Honda. The gunner spread his map on
the turret; they were lost and needed to know the way to
Doc Lap Palace, please. Later, while the journalist was
climbing on the trucks and shaking hands in the crowd, I
thought of the girl. I once knew her when she worked nights
and was familiar with the Palace and its transparencies.
I remembered green tea in bowls pressed with rice grain,
the half moon scar above her eye, and a time when I woke
and saw a strand of her black hair across the pillow and
thought it was the dark blood of the day-old dead. Or the
brush stroke of an inflection that determines the difference

23

between desire and fear. Like something she once taught me
that I've lost in translation. Something as clear as a wind
chime, a symbol of spring offensives, that finally arrives,
shy and unassuming, asking exact directions.

PART TWO

Starting Over: Fortuna, North Dakota

The kamikazes lined up at the bar
Are drinks, not pilots,
Though the effect may be the same.
In the terms of these times,
To be male is to be dead
Or disappointed, to be female
Is to be of many hearts
And alone.
The only juke box in this border town
Repeats like the Divine Wind in my head,
Like the ghosts that still follow Sitting Bull
Along the greasy stones of the Dead River to Canada.
I've come back here to talk
To them or to my own blurred image
Above the back bar about the predetermined –
Of how my life
With its improbable choices
Shouldn't, like the winters,
Go on forever.
There's a woman near here I used to drop in on,
And I remember how once
She pulled her bright kimono tighter
And flipped the butt of my last cigarette
Out an open window. It fell like a small plane,
Like the stone with the seashell fossil in it
I found one time by the Dead River
A thousand miles from the sea.
It's the only thing I ever took
From this place – a kind of proof
That the world can change.

At The Wayne County Fair

I drove all day across this blown-out state
To make it in time for the time trials.
I placed high up on the line for a change
Only to get boxed in by a couple of farm boys
Who race like they're still on the dirt roads
Playing chicken with some jilted sister's
Bad boyfriend. I made a mistake,
Gunned too hard trying to get out
And hit the hay bales at 80 putting the camshaft
Through the fire wall and into the front seat.
It was a good car and now it's lying over there
Off the side of the track
Like a disappointing past
I put a lot into.
Breathing dust in the shade of the grandstand,
I watch the rest of the race
While that girl I picked up in Hagerstown
Is off walking barefoot along the midway,
Or hanging on the sunburned arm of some homeboy
Who's shooting the hell out of
A bunch of plastic ducks,
Going round and round,
Trying to win
Some kind of prize.

Kitchen

I'm snapping wishbones in the widow's kitchen.
I'm wishing against myself,
And each one goes off
With a dry white sound.
The widow sleeps upstairs
While Ernie waits for me
Along the whiplash of sand south of here.
He waits rubbing his tattooed hands
In the cold on the leeside
Of this false dawn.
I'm wasting my time.
Yet Ernie says most things important
Take place in the kitchen,
And after fifteen years in the galley
Of the Aliceanna, he should know.
This house pulls itself
Around that woman upstairs.
In the hallway even the pair of men's boots
And worn-out sou'wester
Sink to the shadows. Last night
In the dance hall the widow
Reached out her strong hand
Leaving a trail of static
From her sweater and hair that said,
This is my place, this is as far
As you go. I took it and felt the bones
In that hand as consistent as the stars,
The streaming moon outside, the thin halyards
Of wind.
Could be, could be, the kitchen seems to sigh
In a flicker of fluorescence,
In disappointment with the familiar
Small things done here each day.
I stack the fractured wish-
Bones in the middle of the widow's hard table
And brush off the eager dust
Their breaking caused.

Working The River

1
I sit on a barge full of shoes.
It belongs to the Valley Line Fleet
From St. Louis.
All the shoes are left-footed.
There is nothing sad about this.

2
In the yellow-green of a southern summer
We are working.
We herd barges like cattle
Or railroad cars. They clang and spark
When they hit the afternoon
That is strange and endless.

3
The river is a metaphor.
It is a dark shriek in the cane
When light clicks.
It is the bad dream, the draw of breath
Across the teeth –
The muscle that moves
An alligator's eye.

4
Covered with grease and oil
We break tow in the sun.
There is the tension of steel cable
In the rocking decks. The water swirls
And my back turns black and shines.
This is the old song and dance
Of nigger work.

5
I eat gravy and rice as evening comes on.
I learn cajun words for women

30

And reluctance. In high river we slide 12 barges
Beneath the Sun Shine Bridge.
Between us and the shore
Is the long reach of isolation
Or marginal error.

Carpenters

The kid from Mississippi takes a shit
in an empty nail box
in the corner of what will soon be the family room.
Brother John signs his name on a rafter
with a flat yellow carpenter's pencil,
and I know we are almost finished with this house.

As frame carpenters we only leave suggestions
for others to follow, completion is not
a responsibility. We are paid to change a plan
into a possibility and for two weeks
a one-hundred-thousand-dollar house is ours.

It must be one hundred on the roof
and even Gene is starting to sweat.
He works along the hip joist carrying a small transistor
tuned to WNEO in New Orleans.
Disco thumps through the white light
of reclaimed swampland, where other houses rise,
and accentuates the sound of hammers.

As frame carpenters we are not concerned
with the finished product or bound by its implications.
Our imaginations are broad enough to see the apparent;
a staircase as only a means of interior support,
a bedroom, a series of right angles.

It is Friday afternoon on the roof of somebody else's house.
The contractors are in town cashing the payroll check,
and on Monday we move to the next lot.
Brother John lights a joint and Gene says that tonight
he's going to stretch out the Buick to Houston.

Factory

– after Liam Rector
(for Jack Stephens)

It all comes down to work.
Honest work like a good vacation.
Working it out with a lover, thinking
ahead and saving work – no worse for wear.
Or working yourself into a frenzy,
"all work and no play makes . . ." etc.
etc. Repetitious work,
over worked,
shit work,
wood work, and
SORRY, NO WORK TODAY. The gray lines break up
into individuals who work their way
home. Alone. Hungry. The inner works.
Work Project Administration.
Working up a sweat while
working your way to the top. How do you like it?
Rehearsing worked-on lines – "On my days off
I like to get out in the yard and work with my hands."
Home work.
Busy work.
Working it into your schedule.
Working on the car, the house, dinner.
"I'm going to work on *her,*" he said with a wink,
his work cut out for him at the bar.
An issue to work around.
The added decisions of a working woman,
worked over.
Worked up. Left for dead or worse,
as when one works under the table, or
works alone in a crowded room,
or works backward, or undercover,
or turns out the light when it doesn't work.

33

Union Town

I must have been sleeping it off in the car
When fall caught up with the hills
Outside of town and streaked them in lines
Of color I took at first
To be the veins of dug out coal.

In town though, it was warm
As we drove past the playground
Of the deaf-and-dumb school and I turned up
The radio until the lyrics
Of a country and western song embarrassed us.
Maybe it was the promise of some safe time
Together, burning like an old matinee
That made us uncomfortable. So you showed me
Around the town where once a lot happened to you
And I understood its easy repetitions to be
Something as familiar to come back to
As another day of work.
A town of fire sales and bad restaurants
Where the retired people all looked a little proud
Of the grey weather, the dead river, the sad zoo.
A town I could have grown up in and so I wanted
To share your urgent affections. I wanted
To hold you the way you wanted to hold on
To a trace of something in your life
That couldn't change.

My hangover wore off in a hotel by the highway
And left me nervous. All night I heard traffic passing
Like the fall coming up behind us.
I felt its cold closing in, moving the burnt air
Under train trestles, and changing
Everything in its way.

At The Bridge Of The Prairie Du Chien

Maybe it is the warm breath of the prairie
Or what follows it,
That brings me here to a place over water.

I've scattered the remnants of other lives
From one shore to the next because
Someone told me this continent
Had no end and I believed her.

Yet there was a city on the edge I revisited
Just to try to walk down one street,
To see for myself the old hotels, the balances
On each end of a turn of events
I might have misunderstood.

Once on a boardwalk, near an ocean whose salt air
Burned my lips, a woman drinking
From a bottle with a shattered neck,
Turned her torn and laughing mouth to me
Saying, "Kiss me, love me."
The clouds muddy the water below. Why would I expect

Anymore, here, in the center of things,
At the Prairie Du Chien where there is just a bridge
And a river – the conditions are clear.
The bridge, a thread loosening in my hands, the river
A needle dipping.

Helicopters

Helicopters patrol your part of the night.
There is no denying them.
You look up as their searchlights wash your face
Like other moons in the sky, and their throb
Is the same throb as your heart.
Once you made love standing up
To a man in an alleyway. You swayed
As thin and durable as the shadows around you.
You could feel them rake the cold pavement.
In your only good dress with street tar
Between your painted toes,
You left trails that were easy to find
And rescue, or search
And destroy.
                        You say never again –
But the young man in uniform who asks you to dance,
Opens his hand like a white flower
That blooms in the night, a moon flower,
And yes, you hear yourself say, and again
the whisper of helicopters.

Suburban Nights

The afternoon leaks into evening.
The rooms go tired one after another
And the stars blow themselves to smithereens
Against the sky. Some scientists
On the news talk about the questions they use
To search space for other life. On a holding pattern
Somewhere above my back yard a stewardess repeats –
Please raise your seat backs to their upright position.
And I slam up straight in my recliner.
There is no other life.
The evening slurs with dilaudid.
The moon is a wound from small arms fire
Turning blue and painful and the circles
That are cigarette burns turn to faces
On my arms. My ex-wife cruises on clover
Leaves west of here and everything spins off kilter.
Wasn't there a drill we used to chant?
Bomb Hanoi/Bomb Saigon/
Bomb Everyone/
And isn't that the way it went?

Variation On A Theme From Tennessee Williams

I wander Decatur Street at dawn
Trying to get to Canal before the sun
Starts to simmer in the Quarter.

Last night we sat on the balcony of the Monteleone,
Ate fish and flipped lit cigarettes into the drunken streets.
Inside the orchestra played oriental foxtrot.
Later I lost you, to the man with the patch
Or the polite negro. It could have been years ago.
I felt your thin wrist slip my grip in the crowd
And a great urgency, not uncommon to these parts,
Rose roaring around me, and carried me
Through the iron-laced night.

Now the sun is up.
Downtown cooks in that awful heat.
I cut across Canal
In my shark-skin suit
Dodging the Desire Street bus.

II
On summer nights we sip beer
In tin-ceilinged bars.
Being a regular is a thankless job.
Here, a blue crack works its way
Along the wall like blood poisoning.
They shore up the piano player
And he begins again.

It is the season for heat lightning.
You mistake my youth for energy
And never shade the lights.
I watch you now in the bar mirror
As your bracelets turn in towards me
Out of focus.
I think of the river nudging into the gulf.

Back outside, a man has stopped
Screaming his wife's name in the street.
You take my arm
And we are ushered in
To the last chance honeymoon dance
At the Fairmont Hotel,
Once called the Roosevelt.

III
When a sense of change
Flicks between the lips
Of flambeaux boys and greying women,
It is usually a matter
Of desire or means.
In this city
Arched beside the river,
Beggars make a choice.

Sidewalks are hosed in front of bars
As shutters spread beneath
The light of another day.
Always, there are rooms of louvered light.
Heat waves rise like birds
From gray pools in the street.

I push my way
Through the flutter of the market.
Everything here is "reach that to me,"
And "let it goes, let it goes cheap."
I buy a newspaper and ease
Into the panic of the crowd,
While you wait in an evening dress
At the Cafe Du Monde.

King Fish

You open your eyes to the clatter of cane
Weaving like sleep across the fields and mud flats
Of river road after a rain.

There is a confusion of smell and sight
And a real need to sit back on some shaded stoop,
To feel the river widen under you
Lifting the green of willows
Reflected in a strand of splitting hair –
A sound that carries.

It is 1935 and every man's a king.
Your hands feel linen and you spit,
Soft-spoken, southern,
Arm-twisted memorabilia.

Small birds sweep by like mistakes
Or a snake shedding skin,
As if there was room for us in remnants
To move between ourselves.
It is that time of year
In this eccentric state.

You rise
In a rattle of sunlight

A man steps out from behind the man
And a screen door swings open
To what the river leaves when it is young
And way beyond itself.

Matthew Brady Speaks Of Whitman

They are slowly emptying the Armory
Square Hospital. I will miss the smell
Of leather and manure the ambulances brought
To F Street each morning. I will not miss
The sawdust or the typhoid.
From my small studio I can see,
Above the cows grazing in the swamp
Of the west lawn, the completed dome
Of the capital. It sits like a lid
Placed atop the rumor and gossip
We depended on so heavily here.
It marks the end
Of a time when this city was mere *idea*
In the eyes of some. A time whose beginnings
I've filed in sections under lovely words
Like Antietam and Manassas; in portraits,
In all the chance moments
That will be labeled history.
Whitman? Yes . . . he was here.
I placed a hat on his head, had him smile,
And suggested he think for a moment
Of immortality. Forgive me, but he sat there
Like a gutted angel.

An Afternoon In Florida

I slip out in the afternoon
And someone takes my picture.

I'm thrown upside down and backwards
Against the ground glass

Of somebody's lens and am caught forever
In this afternoon where the slope of a tiled roof

Above the terrible tunes of a video game
Explains a warm rain gutter that looks

Like the tail pipe of a red Corvette
Just now changing lanes.

This is the afternoon I come back to.
This is the afternoon of the long walk back

To the bad marriage of sea and shore
And the perfect picture postcards I hold.

This morning my own reflection
In the beachwear window where early traffic

Had toppled two mannequins into each others arms
Frightened me again.

The afternoon to come
Would remain as helpless and accidental

As a Cuban wind
Breaking fronds off the Royal Palms,

As the tourist at the end of the boulevard
Snapping pictures of Corvettes that sound much like the sea.

Night Surfing Off Cape Memory

(for Bob Shacochis)

They say the view from there
Is spectacular at dawn,
And you imagine the type of person
Who takes that information at face value;
Shivering along in the chalky light,
Pants rolled up and nothing to see
But dead horseshoe crabs overturned in the rinse.
No, it's from out here that you see that line of land,
Shot through with the Coleman lanterns
Of surf casters and campers,
For what it really is.
It's where you came from.
It's what your shadow on the board will eventually rise to
And rush back toward in starlight over the scalloped
Prairie of the ocean floor.
It's what you'll open up on
Like a fan.

Airport

The airport has its infidelities.
All those arrivals and departures, the delays
and cancellations that seem a way of forgetting
that the airport is merely immediate.
Other places are abstractions. Video reminders
of yesterday and tomorrow.
Here the prevalent thought
is just passing through.
I'm at the airport watching small birds
dart past the plate glass windows
of the observation deck. They bank hard
and dive in formation through the early evening
where huge planes creep.
There is music in the air
at the airport. Lights dance in the boarding gates
and special attention is paid to time.
Jokes are told in the Sky-View Lounge
and the talk at the bar is all casual anticipation.
Transactions are smooth at the airport.

I once knew an artist who painted nothing but ballrooms.
Old hollow ballrooms you could get lost in.
They filled canvases the size of the small rooms
of her studio. The architecture she painted
was a rococo style, florid and nervous, all chocolates
and maroon. Sometimes she added dead palm plants
to the bad light of corners, or perched starlings
in the dust above the silent mezzanines.
Those ballrooms were never meant for dancing.

Who will remember the airport or its possibilities?
The airport has no history.
People lose their way but no one lives in its shadow
or spends long hours conversing
on the concourse, or sleeping on the grassy strip
between runways. The airport exists until the last jet

of the night lifts off leaving landing lights,
someone to sweep up, and the closed ticket booths.
I still have my one small suitcase,
but the bartender stacks glasses anxiously;
everyone at the airport has somewhere else to be.

Beyond The Heartland

It hurt me this morning but I went out
Into the chapped fields to watch the train,
And was left with the taste of thunder
And acetylene.
I think the spray of sunlight
From a silver car can pierce the heart
And pull whole bones from the ground.
I think I was never told the true limits
Of all this endlessness –
The tracks that come to a point, finally,
Beneath birds
Peppering the yellow sky,
The boxcar left behind like a distant room
Where one boy sits humming a song about his home
On carved cliffs above the darkened sea.
            I will go to Kansas City some day.
I will walk in the shadows of great buildings,
And I will see myself as a boy who has come in
From some long hot season
To the protection of a landscape
That is suddenly trainless, cold and predictable,
Almost human.

Trains

Trains couple beneath my bedroom window.
No joke. They disturb my sleep.
I dream train dreams all night
And wake up bothered
By the sadness trains drag
Along that old landscape
Of a dream.
The trains beneath my window *are* a joke.
An odd spur, the dead end
Of a milk run that fakes significance
In its low moan.
Yet mornings, looking over my shoulder,
I walk the tracks, intrigued by diesel scent,
The bits of iron and cloth
That the trains leave behind.

Once I tore my pants and scattered my pack
Over half the Sacramento Valley
Jumping from the Santa Fe Express.
I bounced off into the sunset
To the applause of field hands.
And once a friend and I climbed a westbound car carrier
And rode all night in a new Pinto.
I sat in the back seat
And watched the stars through the sunroof
From the top of the Midnight Limited.

Maybe I should say more.
How these days when waiting alone
At railroad crossings, my head
Full of lights and bells,
I feel I've been waiting all my life.
Or how, when I watch the boxcars
With their awkward freight
Click by like conversations I hardly remember,
I feel they are taking something
Away from me.

California

Sometimes the thought of California
Reminds me of the woman
I never met going west on a train.
I suppose some things must wait.
It's like a nostalgic dream
For something I never had in the past.

Because of this, what is past
Is not always certain. California
Enjoys this dream.
Also there is the woman
Who without realizing it, must wait
For the right time and the right train.

There is something so final about the train.
It comes out of the past
And with it it carries the weight
Of all that we expect of California –
The woman
And the dream.

Believe me, there is much to dream.
Sometimes when I see a train
I, oddly enough, think of a woman
Who is rushing past
To some other place, like California,
Where no one has to wait.

Some of us always have to wait
For the right wind and the right dream.
Yet there are schemes to find California.
The secret is to board a train
That has no use for the past
And gives you a seat next to a woman.

One time I knew a woman.
She used to practice patience by making me wait.

48

I always thought kindly of the past
Until I watched her dream.
Going west on this obsolete train,
If I had one last word it would be California.

Amnesty

I wore a flight jacket once
Torn open all one winter
Because nothing in New York City,
Not the trucks I unloaded,
Or the streets they slammed down,
Was going to touch me.
I thought if I did one or two things right
I might rise above all that business
The way each morning, while I stamped my feet
In the frozen Sea Line Freight Yard,
Sheets of light rose
Above the broken terminals of the Lower Eastside.
I thought, on days there wasn't work,
If I walked Battery Park long enough
Watching two rivers turn into each other,
I might understand what was ahead.
And I thought the habitual Spanish I heard all night
Was just a song a city sang to itself
To soothe the sleep of the girl beside me.
I spent much of my time preoccupied
With birds and the bits of space
Between buildings they disappeared into,
Though it didn't take long
For my hands to clench on their own,
For the wind and the light to blow out
Along the Hudson.

This morning I read a Japanese story
About an old man who lies beside a sleeping girl
And listens to the dry rustle of his heart:
The bad years come back like groves
Of ma-dake; each sharp culm curling
In sea-light, and he finds comfort
In the girl he cannot wake.
I guess it does me no good to go back
To a certain time, the same way I surrender

To a story that is simple and suffocating,
Or to remember, like today, the pale anniversaries
Of moments I gave up. I want to think of the past
As a place I can float above, unmarked,
As a city lit with sleep; where couples walk
The empty avenues, where the rivers are warm,
And the bills of lading lie unused.

Photo by Leslie Adrienne Miller

Matthew Graham was born in the Catskills in 1954. He has received graduate degrees from The Johns Hopkins University and the University of Iowa. He currently teaches at the Indiana State University at Evansville.